Aunt Sue!

I know how much you love dogs, so I thought you would enjoy this book. Thanks again for all you did for Jim and I.

Love you.
Cathy
&
Jim :)

THE Muddiest Buddies

CARPET ONE
FLOOR & HOME

Published by Carpet One Floor & Home
670 North Commercial Street
Manchester, NH 03101

Publisher's Cataloging-in-Publication Data

Carpet One Floor & Home.
    The Muddiest Buddies : A Collection of North America's
Dirtiest Pets / Carpet One Floor & Home.—Manchester, NH :
Carpet One Floor & Home, 2007.

        p. ; cm.
        Includes index.
        ISBN: 978-0-9791546-0-7

        1. Dogs—North America—Pictorial works. 2. Photography
of dogs. I. Title.

    SF430.C37   2007
    636.7—dc22   2006938636

Project coordination by Jenkins Group • www.bookpublishing.com
Cover and interior design and layout by Desktop Miracles, Inc.

Printed in Canada
11 10 09 08 07 • 5 4 3 2 1

THE Muddiest Buddies

A COLLECTION OF NORTH AMERICA'S DIRTIEST PETS

INTRODUCING
North America's Muddiest Buddy ... **Bob!**

Bob, a Yellow Labrador Retriever from Santa Ana, California is the official winner of Carpet One Floor & Home's Muddiest Buddy Contest! At just eight months old, Bob is already gaining fame as the national Lees carpet spokes-pet.

Bob and his owner/breeder, Lauren Bullock, learned about the Muddiest Buddy contest at their local Carpet One Floor & Home store in Corona Del Mar, California. Lauren snapped the winning photo of Bob after he and his six brothers and sisters spent some time playing in the backyard together. At the time, Bob was just eight weeks old!

Bob is friendly, polite, and generally well-behaved with a lovable, outgoing personality to match. But as the muddy photos prove, Bob is also a playful, rambunctious puppy at heart, which can occasionally get him into a bit of harmless trouble!

Lauren entered this adorable photo of Bob, looking a little guilty, in Carpet One Floor & Home's Muddiest Buddy Contest. The photo was chosen from more than 1,000 other entries as one of five finalists. Then it was up to pet-lovers from across North America to choose their favorite Muddy Buddy by voting on CarpetOne.com. Bob won the contest by a landslide, capturing the hearts of hundreds of voters with his mischievous grin.

At five months old, Bob was named the Lees carpet spokes-pet and starred in his own photo shoot. Having his face on the cover of *The Muddiest Buddies: A Collection of North America's Dirtiest Pets* is just the beginning for Bob! As the official Lees spokes-pet, he will be featured in national and local advertising materials for Lees carpet, an extremely stain resistant style that is perfect for Muddy Buddies like Bob!

RelaxitsLees.com

Abby
Golden Retriever
Valparaiso, Indiana

She loves to sneak
up on the bed in
the morning!

Bailey
English Bulldog
Ferndale, Washington

She can swim,
especially in
muddy places.

Chance
Golden Retriever
Bend, Oregon

He obviously
loves to dig!

Buddy

Australian Shepherd

Lithia, Florida

He is a great
Frisbee catcher!

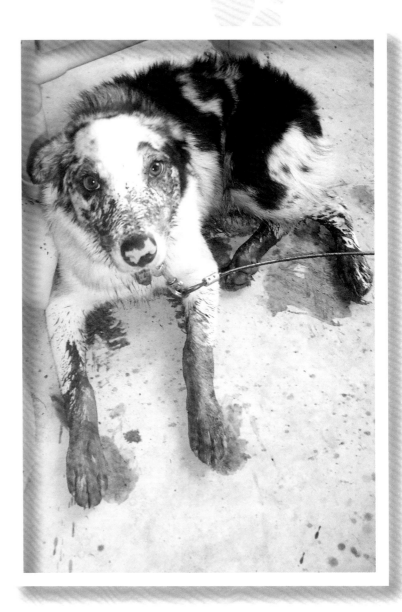

Griffin

West Highland White Terrier

Calgary, Alberta

Loves Scooby Doo!

Charlie
Golden Retriever
Abbottsford, British Columbia

He loves to dive off rocks into the ocean.

Sammy
Golden Retriever
Calgary, Alberta

Grumbles and sighs
to get attention.

Taz
Great Dane
Batavia, Ohio

Loves peanut butter
and mud baths.

Cayenne

Airedale

Mount Laurel, New Jersey

Loves getting wet, digging
and catching moles.

Chelsea

Golden Retriever

Shelby Township, Michigan

She digs in the backyard
for stones!

Cornbread

**Great Pyrenees/
Anatolian Shepherd**

Gassville, Arkansas

Best friends include
a zebra and a
water buffalo.

Zoey
Great Pyrenees
Celeste, Texas

She loves to play
in the water.

Darcy
Yellow Labrador Retriever
Olalla, Washington

Loves to get dirty, play ball and
run through the trees.

Dinger
Great Pyrenees
Roseburg, Oregon

Dinger is a working guard dog with an alpaca farm.

Duggy
Mixed Breed

Calgary, Alberta

Loves the camera
and loves to dig!

Gunny

English Bulldog

Fairhope, Alabama

If there is dirt out there,
Gunny will find it!

Heidi

Scottish Terrier

Jackson, Mississippi

She loves to take your socks off and hide them.

Isabella

Black German Shepherd

Burlington, Washington

She loves mud and snakes.

Julio
Dalmatian
Fountain, Florida

He plays with everyone.

Hank

Yellow Labrador Retriever

Richmond, Virginia

His birthday is on Valentine's Day.

Kodi

Newfoundland

London, Ontario

Despite being 160 pounds, he still tries to sit on laps.

Koko

Rat Terrier

Sheboygan, Wisconsin

Hates thunder storms!

Dora
English Bulldog
Bow, Washington

Likes to root in the mud like a pig.

Lucy
Jack Russell Terrier
Soulsbyville, California

She's CRAZY!

McDuff

**Nova Scotia Duck
Tolling Retriever**

Calgary, Alberta

McDuff has a coat that
sheds dirt quickly. Yes!

Meadow

Yellow Labrador Retriever

Maple Ridge, British Columbia

She thinks she is a lap dog!

Mitzi Million
Yorkshire Terrier
Holts Summit, Missouri

Walks on her hind legs.

Lloyd
Jack Russell Terrier
White Horse Beach, Massachusetts

He's crazy
and loveable.

Maggie

Yellow Labrador Retriever

Wilmington, North Carolina

She is a registered therapy dog.

Morgan

Cocker Spaniel

College Station, Texas

She has a passion for digging. She loves mud!

Muggles

Spinone Italiano

Fairbanks, Alaska

She likes to put her nose on yours and talk to you.

Nikita

Siberian Husky

Newmarket, Ontario

She loves to
run and play!

Bailey

Golden Retriever

Avon, Indiana

Bailey loves to hike and swim!

Lulu

English Bulldog

Oakville, Ontario

She loves toys — the more the better!

Oklahoma

Yellow Labrador Retriever

Cocoa, Florida

Training to be a guide dog.

Orion

American Eskimo/Poodle/Pekingese

Woodbridge, Virginia

He is as crazy as he looks.

Pago
Boxer

Port Townsend, Washington

He loves to bury his toys in mud!

Ralphie
Golden Retriever
Fishers, Indiana

He has a very long tongue!

Rambo

Bichon Shih Tzu

Beiseker, Alberta

He steals people's shoes and hides them in his bed.

Nona

Mixed Breed

House Springs, Missouri

Nona is a pound puppy rescued
at five months of age.

Bentley

Yellow Labrador Retriever

Woodruff, Wisconsin

Loves the camera.

Rocco

Great Pyrenees

Winnipeg, Manitoba

He thinks he is
a lap dog.

Riley | Loves to go swimming
Yellow Labrador Retriever | at the beach!
Bellingham, Massachusetts

Nani
Bernese Mountain Dog
San Diego, California

Loves to swim in the surf.

Samson
Saint Bernard
Ringoes, New Jersey

He loves to mud wrestle with his pal Watson.

Riley

Chocolate Labrador Retriever

Andover, Massachusetts

Riley is obsessed with tennis balls.

Sir Tucker & Queen Ellybelle

Golden Retrievers

Virginia Beach, Virginia

Wild . . . just wild!

Soren

Boxer

Barrie, Ontario

He loves to dig and play with rocks.

Booger

Golden Retriever

Stephenville, Texas

He loves the water!

Tia

Australian Shepherd

Danville, California

She adores California mud baths.

Skipper
Golden Retriever

El Cajon, California

Flew from Boston
to San Diego at
8 weeks old.

Tonka
English Bulldog
Largo, Florida

He loves to sleep.

Tucker

Golden Retriever

Regina, Saskatchewan

He can burp at the most inappropriate times.

Winston

Jack Russell Terrier

Newport, Oregon

It's a good thing he's cute.

Riley

Yellow Labrador Retriever

Etiwanda, California

He likes to bring in
the daily newspaper.

Abby, Shadow & Maggie

Mixed Breeds

El Dorado Hills, California

They are supposed to be
white and fluffy!

Index